To the past, present and future
singers of *Yellow River Cantata*.

GROUNDWOOD BOOKS HOUSE OF ANANSI PRESS

g

TORONTO BERKELEY

A SONG FOR CHINA

HOW MY FATHER WROTE *YELLOW RIVER CANTATA*

ANGE ZHANG

My name is Ange Zhang. I am a Chinese Canadian artist who has lived in Toronto for more than twenty years.

The year 2015 marked the seventieth anniversary of the end of World War II. In commemoration of that event (known in China as the war against the Japanese), *Yellow River Cantata*, a series of songs with lyrics written by my father, Guang Weiran, was performed in many cities in China, as well as in Toronto, Ottawa, New York, Chicago, Los Angeles, Paris, London, Bangkok and Sydney. My family and I attended numerous concerts around the world, and I was invited to give pre-concert talks. There were many children in attendance who fully enjoyed this great piece of music but knew very little about the war in China.

This is the story of *Yellow River Cantata* and the story of my father, who wrote the lyrics.

Above: *Posing in front of a poster for the concert of* Yellow River Cantata *in Chicago.*
Below: *Curtain call, Chicago Symphony Hall, 2015. I am standing fourth from the right at the front of the stage.*

The Yellow River

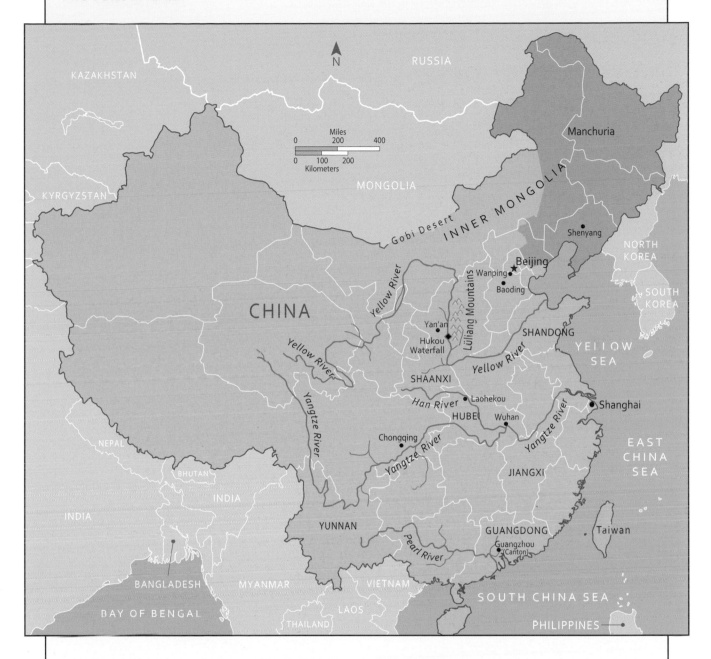

The Yellow River is the Mother River of China and the symbol of Chinese civilization. It is one of China's three most important waterways. The others are the Pearl River and the Yangtze. The Yellow River is the second longest in Asia. It wanders up into Inner Mongolia before emptying into the sea in Shandong province. Ancient Chinese civilization began in its fertile valleys. It has also been called "China's Sorrow" because it has been subject to some of the greatest floods in human history. The deadliest were a 1332–33 flood that killed 7 million people and one in 1887 that was responsible for the deaths of 900,000 to 2 million. The Yellow River has also sometimes changed its course dramatically, affecting millions of people.

All of these events can be explained by the fact that the river carries huge amounts of silt — fine particles of earth — that it accumulates as it flows to the sea. These particles also give the river its distinctive yellow color.

CHILDHOOD

My father was born in 1913 in Laohekou, Hubei province, which is in the middle reaches of the Han River, at the junction of four rivers. Land transportation was also well developed in this area, as it was an important center for material distribution and an ancient strategic military point.

My grandfather, a bookkeeper at a local bank, was an honest man who worked very hard to support his family. He named Father, his first child, Zhang Wenguang — a name that promises a bright literary future.

During his eventful life, Father used more than a dozen different names. Some were pen names, but more often he had to change his name to escape dangerous situations as a result of his involvement in the revolutionary movement. After the success of the revolution, Father started to use the name Zhang Guangnian. However, he is best known by his pen name Guang Weiran, which means a spark that is about to burn brightly.

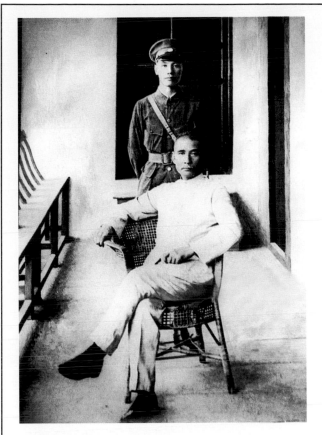

Sun Yat-sen (front) *and Whampoa Military Academy president Chiang Kai-shek at the Whampoa Military Academy.*

China 1910–1915

The year Guang Weiran was born, 1913, Mao Zedong was twenty years old. The last of China's imperial dynasties, the Qing (Manchu) dynasty, had grown increasingly isolated from the people. A feeble six-year-old emperor, Puyi, and his court were opposed by an increasingly vocal group of middle-class reformers and various revolutionary groups, among them the New Army. Sun Yat-sen, one of the dynasty's major opponents, was a Christian who wanted to replace the Empire with a more Western style of government.

By 1911 the Revolutionary Army, which combined Sun Yat-sen's forces with the New Army (in which Mao fought), had overthrown the Qing dynasty, and a Chinese republic led by Sun Yat-sen was created. But in the next few years this government was also overthrown, leading to a major power struggle between political factions.

When he was five years old, Father spent some time at his grandma's home. There was a Daoist temple nearby, and many people went there to burn incense and pray. One day, Grandma took him to the temple to visit a long-bearded priest. The priest looked at the little boy kindly. Then Grandma told Father to kowtow to the priest and to become his apprentice.

From then on, the priest taught Father. His first lesson was the Three Character Classic: "Men at their birth are naturally good. Their natures are much the same; their habits become widely different…"

The family was poor. To save money, Grandfather asked his boss, the banker, to allow Father to accompany the boss's grandson to a private school and to be his "companion boy." Even as a child, Father was smart and sensible, and he loved to read. He read many Confucian classics and could fluently recite hundreds of classic Tang poems. His favorite books were travel books.

The teacher liked this "companion boy" and privately praised him for being meticulous and intelligent, a promising talent.

After a year at the private school, Father went to Laohekou National Primary School. It was the best local experimental school, with a four-year study program equivalent to the normal six-year curriculum. Father had an excellent study record and not only achieved first place in the county graduation exams, but at age eleven, he was the youngest of all the

graduates. Neighbors and family friends came to his home with gongs, drums and a red umbrella to celebrate the good news. Grandfather was happy and proud.

Father attended junior high school when he was twelve years old. Soon after, he learned about the May 30th Massacre.

A 1920s postcard of the Bund, the waterfront area in Shanghai, shown from the French Concession.

On May 15, 1925, a Chinese worker was killed by a Japanese factory owner. Two weeks later, on the morning of May 30, more than two thousand students marched in the Shanghai International Settlement, making protest speeches calling for the government to withdraw all foreign concessions. The police arrested more than one hundred students.

Soon tens of thousands of students and citizens gathered in the British Concession, demanding the release of the arrested students. British police opened fire, killing thirteen people and seriously injuring dozens more.

In the following days, hundreds of thousands of workers, students and businessmen went on strike and joined anti-imperialist demonstrations, calling for the abolition of all foreign privileges in China. The movement soon spread across the country.

Although he was only twelve, Father followed the senior students and actively joined in the local demonstrations. He was very good at public speaking. The students set up a big table on a downtown street. Father stood on it in front of a crowd and called on people to reject Japanese goods and to fight against the oppression by foreign powers.

Drawn to his innocent appearance, his bright voice and his tears of compassion, many people were touched by his speech. This was the first time he participated in a social movement. Father felt deeply that his own fate and that of the Chinese nation were inseparable.

YOUTH

Father's public involvement brought him into a group of aspiring young revolutionaries who often gathered to discuss the future of the country. They treated Father as their little brother, talking about ideas and ways to transform this corrupt society into a new world. For the first time, Father heard the names of Marx and Lenin, and he started to learn about the Chinese Communist Party. Father watched those big brothers and sisters debating. He admired them and wanted to join the revolution to save China. He read many new books and introduced these revolutionary ideas to his fellow junior-high students. He liked Sun Yat-sen's *Three Principles of the People* — nationalism, democracy and the livelihood of the people — and often gathered a group of students in his classroom to recite and explain this book to them.

In 1926, the First United Front, made up of the KMT (Sun Yat-sen's Nationalist Party, the Kuomintang) and the CPC (Communist Party of China), was actively promoting democracy in China. Both the Nationalist and Communist organizations were growing quickly in Hubei. Many enlightened young people became involved in the revolutionary activities, some with the Nationalists, and others with the Communists.

Xiong, a young teacher at Father's school and a core member of the local Communist Party, became Father's good friend. Under his guidance, Father made many speeches at mass rallies, promoting revolutionary ideas to the public and helping his older friends set up a local Nationalist branch in his hometown. Father became the party secretary of the Third Division of the Nationalist Party at Laohekou. His job was to convey the party's directives to more than a dozen members in his branch. Most of them were in their twenties and thirties, yet they were happy to listen to Father, barely a teenager.

One day, Xiong summoned Father to his home and said to him, "You are accepted as a member of the Communist Party of China. We must unite and fight for the future of China. I'm happy to be your sponsor." Father grasped Xiong's hands and held them tight, speechless with excitement.

That evening, thirteen-year-old Father solemnly swore in front of the CPC banner to devote his life to the cause of Communism.

Momentous Years, 1925–1935

Power Struggles, 1925–1934

This was a period of struggle for power between the KMT, the Communist Party of China, various warlords, the colonial powers of France and Britain, and, after 1931, Japan.

Mao Zedong, one of the CPC's founders, was becoming increasingly radical. Although he hoped that the peasantry would become a revolutionary force, he also sometimes collaborated with the Nationalists under Sun Yat-sen.

However, when Sun Yat-sen died in 1925, the KMT was taken over by Chiang Kai-shek, a general who was more conservative and tied to Western interests. On April 12, 1927, he ordered a crackdown on his former Communist allies, assassinating and jailing many of the CPC leaders. In 1930, he was responsible for Mao's wife being killed in front of her eldest son. Mao fled to the mountains in Jiangxi province and spent seven years there, building a disciplined military force. In 1934, Chiang Kai-shek sent a million men to attack Mao, but Mao had already begun to retreat, in what came to be known as the Long March.

Japanese Invasion of China, 1931

In 1931, Japan invaded Manchuria in northern China and set up a puppet state that they called Manchukuo. They installed Puyi, who had been previously deposed as the last Qing emperor, as its ruler. From there they began to take steps to enlarge their domination of northern China.

Communist Party members captured by the army after April 12, 1927.

Cover of the September 1, 1937, issue of the Japanese publication Asahigraph, *featuring Japanese troops marching in northern China.*

(Left to right) *Qin Banxian, Zhou Enlai, Zhu De and Mao Zedong in Yan'an after the Long March.*

Long March, 1934–1935

Mao said, "The Long March is a manifesto. It has proclaimed to the world that the Red Army is an army of heroes, while the imperialists and their running dogs, Chiang Kai-shek and his like, are impotent. It has proclaimed their utter failure to encircle, pursue, obstruct and intercept us. The Long March is also a propaganda force. It has announced to some 200 million people in eleven provinces that the road of the Red Army is their only road to liberation" (*On Guerrilla Warfare*).

The Long March was actually a series of marches by different groups of Communist armies trying to evade destruction by Chiang Kai-shek's much larger military. Led by Mao Zedong, Zhu De and Zhou Enlai, the army made its way from eastern China to the west and north. It ended in Yan'an, in Shaanxi province, on the edge of the Gobi Desert, where Mao consolidated his leadership of the Communist Party of China.

Father often told me that he was both lucky and unlucky in his youth. He was lucky to have lived through the first upsurge of the Chinese revolution, and to be taught revolutionary ideas at an early age. Yet he was unlucky in that soon after he joined the movement, the revolution experienced a disastrous setback. In these years of his adolescence he was surrounded by terror, despair and bewilderment.

In 1927, the right-wing factions in the Nationalist government suddenly turned against the Communists and began a nationwide crackdown on the Party. The Laohekou army opened fire on many Communist members. Local Communist branches disintegrated, as many members either escaped or were arrested and executed, their bodies scattered on the streets of Wuhan. Party organizations began to conduct all their activities in secret. Young and reckless, Father would walk in front of the local army barracks in defiance, with a Manifesto of the Communist Party hidden in his pocket, as if to challenge them.

But soon brutal reality smashed Father's naïve thoughts. He faced a life-or-death fight for survival.

Father described himself as a survivor of these defeats of a great revolutionary movement. The Party did not allow him to participate in the armed revolts because he was still a young teenager. But working as an employee in a bookstore, he was asked to carry out coordination tasks for the Communists using the store as cover. It became a communication center for local Communist branches.

Father was devastated as he watched those who had been so close to him bravely walk to their deaths. Then one day Xiong came to see him. Before he left, he told Father, "I'm going on a long trip. We may not see each other for a while. It's very dangerous out there. Be careful."

Father asked where he was going. Without a word and with tears in his eyes, Xiong suddenly held Father tightly in his arms.

This was the first time Father ever saw Xiong, a tough guy, in tears. He did not realize it was a final farewell until much later, when he learned that his teacher had participated in a peasants' revolt and had been killed by the enemy's machete squad on the shore of the Han River.

The local Communist branches in Laohekou were destroyed. Soon after that, the bookstore where Father worked was shut down after a tip from a traitor. The local army commander summoned Father for an interrogation. Father firmly denied the accusation that he was a member of the Communist Party and said he was only a teenager who had joined the Nationalist Party. Father was already a well-known young poet in his hometown. Even the local army commander had read his classical poems and did not really think he looked like a rebellious figure. So he was given a warning and released.

Seeing Father safely home, Grandfather, who thought he had lost his son forever, scolded him in tears, "Don't ever go out there again. Stay at home and read your books!" Sixteen-year-old Father lost all contact with the Communists. There was no one he could talk to. He hid in a room and shed silent tears for his many close friends and comrades who were dead.

Father was determined to leave his hometown and go to a university in Wuhan. But with what money? To achieve his plan, he first worked as an apprentice at the same bank where Grandfather was a clerk. Then, through a friend, he found a teaching job at a primary school.

In the meantime, he enrolled in correspondence school, studying English and mathematics to prepare for his entrance exams. With his savings and financial support from two older friends and mentors, Father finally had enough money for tuition. In 1932, he went to Wuhan and enrolled in the Department of Chinese Literature at Wuchang University.

At university, Father immersed himself in the study of classical Chinese literature, including *The Book of Odes and Hymns*, *The Songs of Chu* and schools of classical literary criticism. He was also interested in theater and music and participated in discussions and debates on arts, culture and the history of Chinese society. To pay the ten yuan in monthly living expenses, he began to write essays for newspapers and magazines. He wrote on current affairs, as well as reviews of plays and movies. Thus began his career as a professional writer.

Father, 1932

But Father was never one to bury himself in books. During his first year at university, together with a few of his classmates and funded by donations from his fellow townsmen, he set up a quarterly magazine called *Youth of Northern Hubei*, with a printing of a thousand copies. Father was the chief editor, writing literary reviews and commenting on current affairs. The magazine was forced to close after its second edition due to a lack of funding.

During his second year, Father gathered several of his theater-loving friends and set up the Sounds of Autumn Drama Club. The day before their premiere, Father, who had been elected head of the club, announced the play in the *Times Daily* newspaper, using his pen name Guang Weiran for the first time. "We wish to sigh with the autumn wind," he wrote, "or to spread a little warmth with our own enthusiasm… We wish to study life through drama… "

Father failed to complete his final year at the university because he was unable to pay his tuition debt of more than ninety yuan. Through a friend, he found a job at a local high school as a teacher of the Chinese language, while continuing his work as a writer and playwright.

WAR WITH JAPAN

On September 18, 1931, the Japanese army attacked the Chinese army in northeast China using an explosion they themselves had created as a pretext. This became known as the September 18th or Manchurian Incident.

The next day, the Japanese invaded the Manchurian city of Shenyang and gradually occupied the three northeastern provinces. In 1932, the whole territory of northeastern China fell. Japan established a puppet regime, which began fourteen years of enslavement and colonial rule of the people of northeastern China.

Father was in Wuhan. He called on writers to use drama as their weapon to fight for national salvation and freedom from Japan's rule. He and a group of young people established the Pioneer Drama Club, with him as the head of the troupe, the playwright and one of the actors.

He wrote three plays under his pen name Guang Weiran. One of the most popular was *The Girl Named A-Yin*. It's a story about patriotic youth fighting against the Japanese in northeastern China. The musical overture of the play, a song called "Flowers of May," was composed by one of Father's friends.

In 1936, the play was to be performed in Beijing. The theater group there received the script from Father, but for some reason, the score for "Flowers of May" was lost. All they had was the lyrics. So a teacher named Yan Shushi, an exile from northeastern China, composed new music.

"Flowers of May" soon spread throughout China and had a huge influence in the patriotic student movement. You would hear the song wherever there was a national salvation movement action. Rumors spread that the writer of the words was either a martyr or a prisoner. The name Guang Weiran began to be connected to a legendary person.

Father practices singing "Flowers of May" in Shanghai, 1936

The flowers of May are blooming in the field,
Beneath the flowers the patriot's blood is flowing...

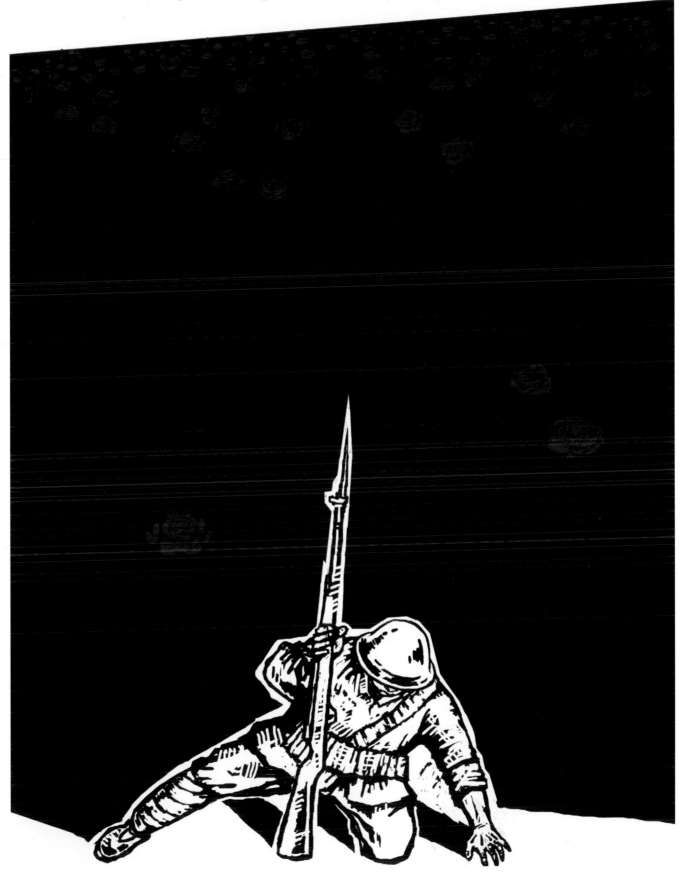

In 1936, Father was twenty-three years old. In addition to the drama club, he also ran a reading club. There were two hundred members, most of them young people who yearned for reform.

Because of Father's revolutionary activities and growing reputation, the Nationalist government decided to arrest him. A Communist Party member heard the news and urged Father to escape from Wuhan to Shanghai. He immediately packed a small suitcase and went to the ferry.

When he learned he would have to wait ten hours before the ferry's departure, he decided to return to the city and visit a friend. They ate dinner and saw a movie.

When Father returned to the ferry half an hour before its departure, he realized that he had had a lucky escape from the police. They had searched his home and the ferry while he was in the city with his friend.

On July 7, 1937, the Japanese army attacked the Chinese army stationed at Marco Polo Bridge in Wanping just southwest of Beijing. Following a Japanese victory on the bridge and the Chinese army's retreat to Baoding, the Beijing area fell into Japanese hands. The July 7th Incident precipitated events that led to all-out war for China and the beginning of the Eastern Front of World War II.

Having arrived in Shanghai, Father formed another reading club to advocate for anti-Japanese national salvation. In the meantime, he was actively involved in the Shanghai theater world. To make a living, he worked as a freelance movie and theater critic. His English was passable and sometimes, when a new English movie opened, he fought to get into the first showing so he could write a review right away for the evening newspapers. He and his roommates — a film actor, a playwright and a translator — practiced a Communist way of life, sharing their food and money, and sometimes even their clothes. They would all go to a restaurant to celebrate whenever one of them was paid.

Young, charismatic and a good communicator, Father drew many like-minded people to him wherever he went. They liked and trusted him. He soon gathered a group of idealistic artists and writers, and Guang Weiran became very well known among the literary and artistic circles of Shanghai.

Top: *Father in Shanghai, 1936*

Below: *Father performing on stage in Shanghai, 1936*

Opposite: *Japanese troops enter Beijing Qianmen Street in late July 1937.*

Lyrics for "Flowers of May" written by Guang Weiran, 1936

One summer day in 1937, Father led thirty friends from his reading club to a suburb for a national salvation cultural activity. Thousands of young people there were learning a song. When Father arrived, he realized that the well-known composer Xian Xinghai was teaching people to sing "Flowers of May."

Even though Father and Xian Xinghai had heard of each other, they had never met. During the break, one of Father's friends shouted, "The writer is here! Guang Weiran is here!" Father was pushed onto the stage. Xian Xinghai shook his hands excitedly and asked him to give a speech.

Xing Xinghai invited Father to his home, showed him his music and shared his ideas. They had so much in common that they decided to work together to write a musical commemorating the Russian writer Maxim Gorky. It was to be performed the following week, so the two completed their first joint work, *Song of Maxim Gorky*, that very evening.

A few months later, the Japanese occupied Shanghai. Father and many other members of the artistic community evacuated to central China.

In response to the Japanese invasion, the Nationalist and Communist forces decided to join again and formed the Second United Front. In 1938, under the leadership of the Communist Party, the Third Division of the Political Department of the National Military Committee was established in Wuhan, and Father was appointed an officer of the theater section with a major rank. He was responsible for organizing ten theater troupes and one children's theater troupe for the resistance movement. He and his friends from the Communist Party completed the task in a few months. Around three hundred young artists from different cities and different family backgrounds joined the troupes, all eager to go to the anti-Japanese battlefront. The troupe members were not only required to sing and perform, but the men had to learn to use weapons, and the women first-aid skills. The young artists said farewell to their loved ones, determined to devote their lives to the defense of their country.

Above: *Father gives a speech in front of theater troupe members, 1938*

Right: *Father in military uniform, 1938*

Following the fall of Shanghai, Wuhan became the new cultural center of China. Prominent figures from music and the arts gathered there. Among them were many of Father's friends from Shanghai.

Meanwhile, Xian Xinghai was also hired by the Third Division of the Political Department, responsible for organizing anti-Japanese singing groups in Wuhan. The two old friends were happily reunited. This time they even shared a room, sleeping in bunk beds. They were both very busy in their own work and hardly saw each other during the day. But they managed to write songs at night. If there was going to be an important event, they would write a song to give it a boost. Often the rehearsal or mass rally took place the next day. If Xian came home and found Father asleep, Xian would wake him up, saying, "Hurry up! You have to write something!" Father would write the words right away, and Xian would finish the music overnight and teach it to the masses the next morning.

They composed more than ten songs together during these sleepless nights. One of them was "Defend Greater Wuhan," which was sung by hundreds of thousands of people during the Battle of Wuhan.

The Japanese army captured Wuhan in October 1938 after four months of fighting. While the Chinese Air Force and Navy had taken significant hits, the land force was still mostly intact. However, the Japanese army was weakened, which bought the Chinese forces more time to prepare for an extended war of resistance.

Chinese soldiers in the Battle of Wuhan in September 1938.

In the autumn of 1938, in the heat of the war against the Japanese army, Father was appointed Publicity Commissioner of the Northwestern Battle Zone. He was to lead a group of young performing artists to Shanxi province, where the Chinese army was fighting, using the natural barrier provided by the great Yellow River.

The group visited the battlefront repeatedly over a few months and saw many heroic acts by militiamen and soldiers. Father could not help but use his weapon — the pen — to praise the heroes. He wrote a single-act play called *Raise Your Weapons*, which became part of the regular repertoire for his troupe.

Late in October 1938, Father and his troupe were traveling along the Yellow River valley, seeking to cross it to join the anti-Japanese militia base in the Lüliang mountains.

With loud rumbling and the sight of rising mist ahead of them, they eagerly came around a bend and suddenly saw the spectacular Hukou waterfall in front of them.

Overwhelmed by the massive power of nature with the water roaring like thunder in front of him, Father stretched out his arms and shouted, "Ah, Yellow River," as if he were a poet on stage. With inspiration and passion burning like a fire, he decided then and there to write a set of poems to express his admiration for the great Mother River of China.

Father (middle) *with soldiers and crew members in the Lüliang mountains guerrilla zone in 1938.*

On November 1, 1938, Father and his troupe got ready to cross the Yellow River on a ferry. They boarded a large square wooden boat. Forty half-naked boatmen jumped into the water and pushed the boat into the raging deep river. Then they jumped back onto the boat one by one and positioned themselves evenly on both ends like soldiers. The chief helmsman, a white-bearded old man, shouted the boatmen's chant. The crew repeated his tune and moved in rhythm with his command.

As the boat approached the treacherous mid-stream, the rhythm of the chant became faster, the pitch higher, and the volume louder and stronger. On the boat, Father experienced this so powerfully that he felt he was fighting the raging waves along with the boatmen. The thrilling scene shook him to the core. In the wild power of the Yellow River, he saw the great courage of the Chinese people. This was what he had been looking for — his nation's heroic spirit, great and strong!

That day happened to be Father's twenty-fifth birthday.

YELLOW RIVER CANTATA

On his way back from an anti-Japanese militia base in January 1939, Father's horse suddenly went out of control and threw him on a rocky shore. The fall shattered his left elbow. No doctor could be found in that remote mountainous area, so his comrades and villagers carried him on a stretcher over hundreds of kilometers to a hospital in Yan'an. From 1935 to 1948, the headquarters for the Communist Party were in Yan'an. The Party had arrived there over the course of the Long March.

As it happened, Xian Xinghai was in Yan'an as the head of the music department of Lu Xun Academy of Arts. When he heard that Guang Weiran was recovering from an injury nearby, he immediately went to the hospital. The two friends were so happy to see each other again. They talked about a new era in China and about the war. They wanted to work together again to create something exciting.

Lying in bed after Xian Xinghai had left, Father was unable to contain his thoughts. In the past few months, while trekking in the anti-Japanese battle zone along the Yellow River, he had gathered so much first-hand experience about the Chinese people in war. He decided to use this material to write a chorus suite. Unable to use his hand because of the injury, he recited the words while an artist in his troupe recorded it on paper. Father immersed himself in a creative world, his spirit soaring and his verses pouring out like the waves of the Yellow River.

Within five days, the lyrics for *Yellow River Cantata* — eight movements, including a 130-line recital movement — were complete!

Left: *Father in Chongqing, 1940*

Middle: *Father at Yan'an Hospital, 1939*

Right: *Xian Xinghai in Yan'an with his wife and daughter, 1939*

Father (back row, third from left) *and members of the Third Division in Yan'an, 1939*

On the evening of March 11, 1939, Father recited the poem to more than thirty artists in a spacious cave dwelling at Yan'an Northwest Hotel. Xian Xinghai was seated by the door. Standing under the kerosene lamp, his left arm in a sling, Father described the background and the structure of his *Yellow River Cantata*. Then he started the recital: "Dear friend, have you seen the Yellow River? Have you crossed the Yellow River? Do you remember the boatmen risking their lives to battle the perilous waves?"

Everyone in the hall was thrilled when Father finished the last line. Xian Xinghai jumped up, grabbed the sheets from his hand and said, "I promise I will make a good piece of music out of it!"

The Yellow River, the Mother River of China, had inspired Guang Weiran. His words deeply moved Xian Xinghai, and now it was his turn to create great music for it. Xinghai had studied music in France, where he loved to eat candy while he worked. My father would search everywhere for small amounts of pure sugar (which was not easy to find in Yan'an), and he would give this to his friend and collaborator to inspire him while he composed.

Sharing the same passion and dreams for China's future, the young poet and young composer used their own weapons to fight against the Japanese invasion.

Xian Xinghai began to compose the music. In just six days and nights, on March 31, 1939, *Yellow River Cantata*, an epic musical work, was completed.

In a remote country town like Yan'an, western musical instruments were hard to find. Xian Xinghai tried to write music for the musical instruments that were available there, including Chinese instruments and even household objects. His orchestra had three violins, as well as erhu, sanxian, flute, guitar, harmonica and drums. One of the bass huqin was made by his students using a kerosene barrel. He also put spoons into a big enamel cup as a percussion instrument. Xinghai cleverly used these instruments to create a piece of music with both Chinese and Western elements, adding rich national color to the orchestra.

Xian Xinghai composes in a cave in Yan'an, 1939

wood block

harmonica

drum

allegro

cymbals

guitar

bell

gong

bamboo flute

hand-made percussion instrument

violin

sanxian

big sanxian

hand-made bass huqin

erhu

Yellow River Cantata premiered on April 13, 1939, at Shanbei Gonxue Hall of Yan'an. The house was full that night. Mao Zedong and other leaders came to the concert.

The curtain went up. The first movement, "Song of the Yellow River Boatmen," grabbed the audience's attention immediately. The choir and the orchestra presented a powerful image on stage.

The third spoken movement, "Yellow River from Heaven Descends" was presented by Father himself, accompanied by a shamisen. A spotlight shone on Father, who was wearing a black cloak to cover his injured left arm. He looked very handsome on stage. The audience was taken on an emotional journey.

The climax of the concert was the seventh movement, "Defend the Yellow River." With its powerful and triumphant choral music, it expressed the will and determination of the Chinese people to defend their motherland against the enemy.

Before the performance of Yellow River Cantata, *Xian Xinghai (sixth from left, front row) is shown with members of the band and choir.*

Left: A children's choir rehearses Yellow River Cantata.

Middle: Members of the Third Division rehearse Yellow River Cantata.

The first performance of *Yellow River Cantata* in Yan'an was an unprecedented success. Since then, the cantata has represented the voices of the Chinese nation. Its waves echoed across the northern and southern banks of the Yellow River, inside and outside the Great Wall, and throughout the anti-Japanese battlefields to the whole of China.

Xian Xinghai conducts Yellow River Cantata *in Yan'an, 1939.*

On October 1, 1949, Mao Zedong announces the founding of the People's Republic of China.

World War II in China and the Triumph of the Chinese Revolution in 1949

After Japan launched a full-scale invasion of China in 1937, a temporary truce was established between Chiang Kai-shek's forces and the Red Army to jointly fight the Japanese. But once Japan lost the war in 1945, the struggle between the Communists and the Nationalists, who were backed by the United States, resumed. In 1949, the Red Army finally defeated the Nationalists, who fled to Taiwan and set up a government there under Chiang Kai-shek.

And the People's Republic of China, under Mao Zedong and the Communist Party of China, was established.

Father (front) parading through Yangon as a leader of the Myanmar Overseas Chinese Wartime Task Force, 1941

Left: *Father in Yunnan, 1942*
Right: *Father and Mother in Beijing, 1950*

EPILOGUE

After leaving Yan'an, Father continued his cultural and arts activities in Chongqing, Myanmar, Yunnan and Beijing. Father and Mother were married in Beijing in 1946. After the establishment of the People's Republic of China in 1949, Father became a senior official in charge of the theater, arts and literature sectors successively, while he continued to write poems and literary reviews. During the Cultural Revolution (1966–1976), he was stripped of all his duties and sent to a labor camp in southern China. The lyrics of *Yellow River Cantata* were criticized and banned.

In 1946, Father and Mother married in Beijing. Many Communists from cultural circles attended the wedding. It became a social gathering to protest against the ruling government.

But in September 1975, on the thirtieth anniversary of Xian Xinghai's death, *Yellow River Cantata* was finally allowed to be performed again. Soon after that, Father was reinstated to his former position and returned to Beijing. As one of the central policy-makers in that area, he made important contributions to the restoration and development of Chinese literature.

After retirement, he devoted his time to writing. In his late eighties, he published a five-volume collection of his own writing as well as a translation of the great Chinese classic by Liu Xie (AD 465–520), *The Literary Mind and the Carving of Dragons (Wen Xin Diao Long)*, one of the most important works of Chinese culture. Father worked from 1960 until 2000 on a translation that restored the harmony of the original text and is considered unique.

Father passed away in 2002. His ashes were scattered in the upper reaches of the Yellow River by his loved ones.

Father in his home in Beijing in 1998

Opposite: *The first English edition of* Yellow River Cantata, *published in 1946 by Leeds Music Corporation in New York.*

yellow river cantata

music by Hsu Hsing-hai

text by Kwang Wei-yuan

1.00
IN U.S.A.

LEEDS MUSIC CORPORATION
RADIO CITY • NEW YORK

yellow river cantata
for chorus, soloists and narrator

text by Kwang Wei-yuan
music by Hsu Hsing-hai

adapted for American use by
Wallingford Riegger

1. chant of the yellow river boatmen
chorus

VOICE: Friends! Have you ever seen the Yellow River?
Have you crossed the Yellow River?
Do you remember the scene as the boatmen fought
a life-and-death battle against the swift currents
and high waves?
If you have forgotten, listen to this:

＊"Uh-ya," as if in great exertion from rowing.

1. Song of the Yellow River Boatmen

Recitation
Dear friend, have you seen the Yellow River?
Have you crossed the Yellow River?
Do you remember the boatmen
risking their lives to battle the perilous waves?
If you have forgotten,
then listen!

Chorus
Hai-yo! Row!
Row, forge ahead! Hai-yo!
Stormy clouds veil the sky;
waves surge high as mountains;
cold wind stings our faces;
surf crashes into the boat.
Fellow boatmen, keep a lookout.
Helmsman, hold firm.
Stay alert, do not take chances.
Fight for your lives, do not be afraid.
Hai! Row!
Fear not the mountainous waves.
Boating on the river is like fighting on the front line;
rally together, forward we go. Hai! Row!
Row, forge ahead. Hai-yo! Hahaha!
The shore is in our view,
the shore is under our feet.
Calm our hearts down
and catch a breath.
Then once again, we will risk our lives fighting those raging waves.
Hai-yo! Row! Hey!

2. Ode to the Yellow River

Recitation
Ah, my friends.
The heroic spirit of the Yellow River
dominates the plains of Asia.
It is the spirit of our nation,
mighty and strong.
Here, in front of the Yellow River,
we sing our praise.

Aria
Standing on the mountaintop,
I see the Yellow River rolling toward the southeast.
Golden waves surge, lofty waters rise;
muddy swirling rapids mark its sinuous course
rushing from the Kunlun Mountains to the Yellow Sea,
dividing the central plains of China
into southern and northern halves.
Ah, Yellow River, you are the cradle of the Chinese nation.
You have nurtured five thousand years of ancient culture;
many heroic acts have taken place on your shores!
Ah, Yellow River, you are mighty and strong,
like a giant appearing on the plains of Asia.
Your majestic physique is our nation's defense.
Ah, Yellow River, you rush along to the horizon,
majestic, extending your arms like countless strips of iron
toward northern and southern shores.
Our nation's great spirit
will flourish under your nurture!
From you, our homeland's heroic sons and daughters will learn
to become as mighty and strong as you!

3. Yellow River from Heaven Descends

Recitation
Yellow River, we wish to become
mighty and strong like you!
Here, we offer a poem,
confiding in you the catastrophes suffered by our people.

Recitation, accompanied by the Chinese musical instrument, the sanxian
Yellow River descends from heaven –
sweeping, surging forward.
The cries of the raging river will shake you to the core!
It is China's major artery,
circulating the nation's lifeblood throughout the land.
The sun shines high; golden rays burst from the waves.
The moon rises over the eastern mountains;
silver reflections glimmer like snow.

The river shakes and leaps
like a flying dragon,
traversing thousands of miles a day,
diving into the vast eastern sea.

Hukou Falls and Longmen Gorge
form a magical display.
No one dares to lean close to the riverside;
even a ferocious dragon
would not dwell on the riverbed.

From miles away,
you can see the thick plumes of smoke rising
as if from a large blazing fire, spreading over the entire sky.
The sight will make your blood boil;
then the chilled air will blow in,
and you will tremble with cold.

The river groans and quakes,
emitting the power of a billion horses,
shaking the Earth's crust
and dispersing the dark clouds in the sky.

Ah, Yellow River, the king of rivers!
When enraged, it is a wild beast,
fiercer than thousands of poisonous pythons;

making waves, stirring up storms
and wrecking man-made embankments.

Hence, on both shores of the Yellow River,
terrible calamities took place:
the river devoured lives
and leveled villages across hundreds of miles.
Tens of thousands of survivors, old and young,
were exiled to the unfamiliar land,
starving, hanging on the verge of death.

Today, people along the riverbanks are once again
suffering unprecedented calamities:
the pirates from the East are letting out murderous fumes of death
on Asia's vast plains;
starvation and death are like a contagious fever,
spreading on the shores.

Ah, Yellow River!
You have nurtured our nation's growth.
You have also witnessed
the calamities China has suffered for five thousand years!

Countless bloody battles have unfolded
on the shores of the Yellow River.
Piles of white bones fill your depths;
streams of blood stain your surface!

Yet, you have never seen
brutality like this unleashed as it is now by the
    invaders;
nor have you seen the Yellow Emperor's sons and
    daughters
mobilize the entire country as they do today.

On the shores of the Yellow River,
militia groups and army troops
are scattered like stars, spreading out behind the
    enemy lines;
in the green crop fields and mountain valleys,
valiant battles are launched!

Ah, Yellow River!
You record our nation's history through the
    dynasties;
from the past to the present,
many heroes rose along your banks!

Yet, never before have you seen
four hundred million fellow countrymen
united as steel and iron.
Hundreds of thousands of heroes
spill their blood to defend our motherland;
their heroic tales are like your raging waves,
strong, intense and magnificent!

Ah, Yellow River!
Can you hear victory's songs
prevail on your shores?

Can you see the iron army of our nation
spreading out like a net
that covers the earth and the sky?

They guard your shores
against the ferocious enemy
and bury them
beneath your billowing waves!

Ah, Yellow River!
You rush and roar,
ridding the country of the fascists' demons,
singing their burial song!

Your deafening roar
echoes across our land,
a triumphant song to honor our people's great
    victory!
Roar out loud across our land,
a triumphant song to honor our people's great
    victory!

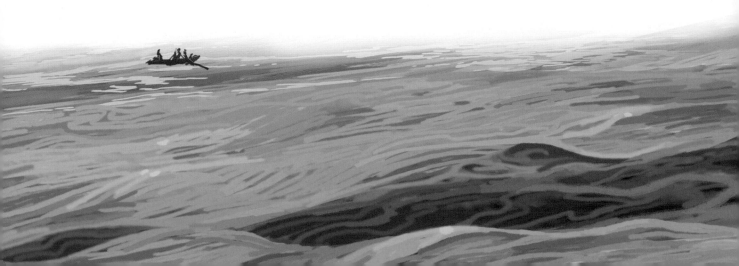

4. Yellow Water Ballad

Recitation
We are sons and daughters of the Yellow River,
who arduously strive toward victory with each passing day!
But each day that the enemy is not destroyed
is one more day that we cannot rest.
If you doubt this,
then listen to the painful groans of the multitudes of people east of the river.

Chorus
Yellow waters rush eastward.
They flow for ten thousand miles.
Swift currents, rolling waves,
roaring like a tiger.
The people opened canals and built dams
to the east where level and fertile soil lies;
the wheat seedlings plump, the beans sweet.
Men and women, young and old,
were radiant with joy.
But since the enemy came,
the people have suffered.
Rape and slaughter
have left a trail of desolation.
Bringing their old and young, the people flee to seek refuge.
They lose fathers and mothers along the way; they have no homes to return to!
Yellow waters rush along day and night
as families are torn apart.

5. A Dialogue on the River Bank

Recitation
Families torn apart, wives without husbands, children
    without parents!
Will we be homeless forever?
Listen to two villagers talk on the bank of the Yellow
    River.

Duet
A: Zhang Laosan, may I ask you,
where is your hometown?
B: My home is in Shanxi,
three hundred miles across the river.
A: In your hometown,
did you farm the land or trade?
B: I held the hoe, plowed the fields, planted sorghum
    and millet.
A: Why, then, are you here,
wandering the river bank, lonely and sorrowful?
B: Please don't bring up painful matters.
My home was destroyed and I know not the fate of
    my family.
A: Zhang Laosan, don't be sad.
My fate is worse than yours!
B: Why, Wang Laoqi, where is your hometown?
A: I used to trade in the northeast;
for eight long years I've had no news from home.
B: All this said, you and I
both have homes we can't return to!

A and B Duet
Within our hearts, enmity and hatred swirl
like the rapids of the Yellow River.
On the river's bank, let us resolve to fight back!
For our country, we will become fighters,
go up the Taihang Mountains and fight as guerrillas.
From this day on, you and I
together will fight to regain our homeland!

6. Yellow River Lament

Recitation
Friends! We will fight and regain our homeland!
Our country is in such disarray!
We all have families!
How can we bear the humiliation from the invaders?
Dear compatriots,
listen to a woman's sorrowful song.

Aria
Oh, wind, do not howl.
Oh, clouds, do not hide.
Yellow River, do not whimper!
Tonight, I stand before you, weeping,
to pour out my hatred and grief.
Oh, fate, so bitter. Oh, life, so hard.
Invaders, you are so evil!
My precious child died so horribly!
The cruelty you forced onto me
took away my will to live in this world.
Oh, wind, do not howl.
Dark clouds, do not hide.
Yellow River, do not whimper.
Tonight, I will throw myself into your embrace
to end my deep sorrows and sufferings!
My husband, who is beyond the horizon;
in death we shall be reunited.
Remember the tragic deaths of your wife and child.
You must settle this blood debt!
You must avenge your family!

7. Defend the Yellow River

Recitation
Sons and daughters of China,
who wants to be slaughtered like sheep?
We must resolve to fight for victory!
To defend the Yellow River!
To defend the north!
To defend all of China!

Chorus
The wind howls, horses neigh,
the Yellow River roars!
To the west stands a towering hill;
to the east and north, sorghum has ripened.
Amid thousands of mountain clusters are many heroes.
Inside green curtains of tall crops,
valiant guerrilla warriors fight.
Armed with home-made weapons
and foreign guns,
waving machetes and spears,
they defend their hometowns!
Defend the Yellow River!
Defend northern China!
Defend all of China!

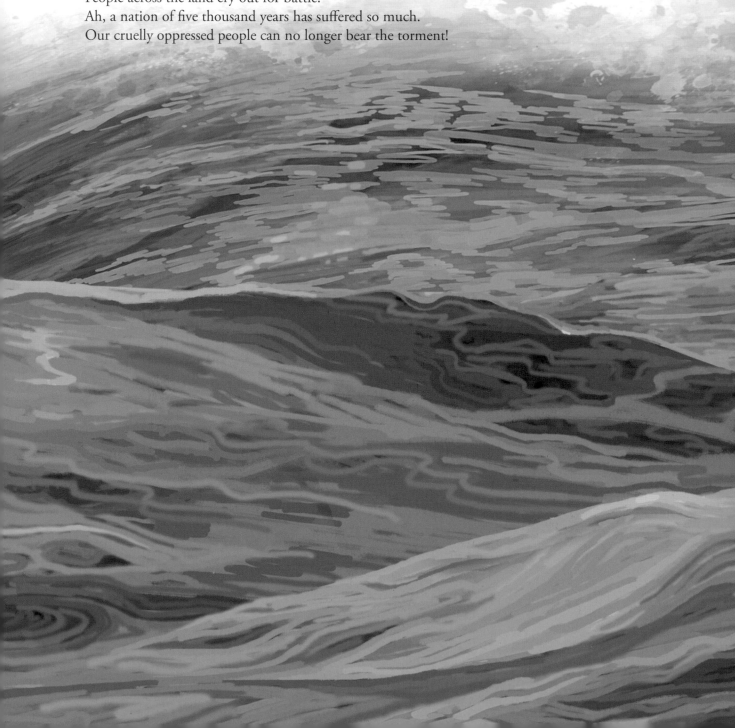

8. Roar, Yellow River!

Recitation
Listen, the Pearl River roars!
The Yangtze River is raging on!
Ah! Yellow River.
Raise up your angry waves, let loose your wild bellows;
sound the battle cry for all oppressed people of China.
Sound the battle cry!

Chorus
Roar, Yellow River!
Raise up your angry waves, let loose your wild bellows!
People across the land cry out for battle!
Ah, a nation of five thousand years has suffered so much.
Our cruelly oppressed people can no longer bear the torment!

For China, a new dawn is appearing;
four hundred and fifty million people have united,
pledging their lives to defend this land.
Listen, Songhua River is calling;
Heilong River is calling;
the mighty Pearl River roars its defiance;
along the Yangtze River, all beacon lights are burning!
Ah! Yellow River! Roar on!
Sound the battle cry
to the suffering people of China!
Sound the battle cry
to all the people of the world!

黄河大合唱 (歌词八首)

一 黄河船夫曲（男生合唱）

（朗诵词）
朋友！
你到过黄河吗？
你渡过黄河吗？
你还记得河上的船夫
拼着性命和
惊涛骇浪搏战的情景吗？
如果你已经忘掉的话，
那么你听吧！

（歌词）
咳哟！
划哟！划哟！划哟！
划哟！冲上前！
划哟！冲上前！……
咳哟！
乌云啊，遮满天！
波涛啊，高如山！
冷风啊，扑上脸！
浪花啊，打进船！
咳哟！
伙伴啊，睁开眼！
舵手啊，把住腕！
当心啊，别偷懒！
拼命啊，莫胆寒！
咳！划哟！
咳！划哟！
不怕那千丈波浪高如山！
不怕那千丈波浪高如山！
行船好比上火线，
团结一心冲上前！
咳！划哟！
咳！划哟！
咳哟！划哟！……
划哟！冲上前！
划哟！冲上前！……
咳哟！

哈哈哈哈……！
我们看见了河岸，
我们登上了河岸，
心啊安一安，
气啊喘一喘.
回头来，
再和那黄河怒涛
决一死战！
决一死战！

二 黄河颂 （男声独唱）

（朗诵词）
啊，朋友！
黄河以它英雄的气魄，
出现在亚洲的原野；
它表现出我们民族的精神：
伟大而又坚强！
这里，
我们向着黄河，
唱出我们的赞歌。

我们祖国的英雄儿女，
将要学习你的榜样，
像你一样地伟大坚强！
像你一样地伟大坚强！

（歌词）
我站在高山之巅，
望黄河滚滚，
奔向东南。
惊涛澎湃，
掀起万丈狂澜；
浊流宛转，
结成九曲连环；
从昆仑山下，
奔向黄海之边；
把中原大地
劈成南北两面。
啊，黄河！
你是中华民族的摇篮！
五千年的古国文化，
从你这儿发源；
多少英雄的故事，
在你的身边扮演！
啊，黄河！
你是伟大坚强，
像一个巨人
出现在亚洲平原之上，
用你那英雄的体魄
筑成我们民族的屏障。
啊，黄河！
你一泻万丈，
浩浩荡荡，
向南北两岸
伸出千万条铁的臂膀。
我们民族的伟大精神，
将要在你的哺育下
发扬滋长！

三 黄河之水天上来 （朗诵歌曲）

(朗诵词)
黄河!
我们要学习你的榜样,
像你一样地伟大坚强.
这里,
我们在你面前,
献上一首诗,
哭诉我们民族的灾难.

(歌词)
黄河之水天上来,
排山倒海,
汹涌澎湃,
奔腾叫啸,
使人肝胆破裂!
它是中国的大动脉,
在它的周身,
奔流着民族的热血.
红日高照,
水上金光迸裂.
月出东山,
河面银光似雪.
它震动着,
跳跃着,
像一条飞龙,
日行万里,
注入浩浩的东海.
虎口——龙门,
摆成天上的奇阵;
人,
不敢在它的身边挨近;
就是毒龙
也不敢在水底存身.
在十里路外,
仰望着它的浓烟上升,
像烧着漫天大火,
使你热血沸腾;
其实——
凉气逼来,
你会周身感到寒冷.
它呻吟着,
震荡着,

发出十万万匹马力,
摇动了地壳,
冲散了天上的乌云.
啊,黄河!
河中之王!
它是一匹疯狂的猛兽啊,
发起怒来,
赛过千万条毒蟒,
它要作浪兴波,
冲破人间的堤防;
于是黄河两岸,
遭到可怕的灾殃:
它吞食了两岸的人民,
削平了数百里外的村庄,
使千百万同胞
扶老携幼,
流亡他乡,
挣扎在饥饿线上,
死亡线上!
如今
两岸的人民,
又受到空前的灾难:
东方的海盗,
在亚洲的原野,
放出杀人的毒焰；
饥饿和死亡,
像黑热病一样,
在黄河的两岸传染!
啊,黄河!
你抚育着我们民族的成长;
你亲眼看见,
这五千年的古国
遭受过多少灾难!
自古以来,
在黄河边上
展开了无数血战,
让累累白骨
堆满你的河身,
殷殷鲜血
染红你的河面!
但你从没有看见

敌人的残暴
如同今天这般；
也从没有看见
黄帝的子孙
像今天这样
开始了全国动员；
在黄河两岸，
游击兵团，
野战兵团，
星罗棋布，
穿插在敌人后面；
在万山丛中，
在青纱帐里，
展开了英勇的血战!
啊,黄河!
你记载着我们民族的年代,
古往今来,
在你的身边
兴起了多少英雄豪杰!
但是,
你从不曾看见
四万万同胞
像今天这样
团结得如钢似铁；
千百万民族英雄,
为了保卫祖国
洒尽他们的热血；
英勇的故事,
像黄河怒涛,
山岳一般地壮烈!
啊,黄河!
你可曾听见
在你的身旁
响彻了胜利的凯歌?
你可曾看见
祖国的铁军
在敌人后方
布成了地网天罗?
他们把守着黄河两岸,
不让敌人渡过!

他们要把疯狂的敌人
埋葬在滚滚的黄河!
啊,黄河!
你奔流着,
怒吼着,
替法西斯的恶魔
唱出灭亡的葬歌!
你怒吼着,
叫啸着,
向着祖国的原野,
响应我们伟大民族的
胜利的凯歌!

四 黄水谣 （齐唱）

（朗诵词）
我们是黄河的儿女!
我们艰苦奋斗,
一天天地接近胜利.
但是,
敌人一天不消灭,
我们一天便不能安身;
不信,你听听
河东民众痛苦的呻吟.

（歌词）
黄水奔流向东方,
河流万里长.
水又急,
浪又高,
奔腾叫啸如虎狼.
开河渠,
筑堤防,
河东千里成平壤.
麦苗儿肥啊,
豆花儿香,
男女老少喜洋洋.
自从鬼子来,
百姓遭了殃!
奸淫烧杀,
一片凄凉,
扶老携幼,
四处逃亡,
丢掉了爹娘,
回不了家乡!
黄水奔流日夜忙,
妻离子散,
天各一方!
妻离子散,
天各一方!

五 河边对口曲 （对唱）

（朗诵词）
妻离子散,
天各一方!
但是,
我们难道永远逃亡?
你听听吧,
这是黄河边上
两个老乡的对唱.

（歌词）
张老三, 我问你,
你的家乡在哪里?
我的家, 在山西,
过河还有三百里.
我问你, 在家里,
种田还是做生意?
拿锄头, 耕田地,
种的高粱和小米.
为什么, 到此地,
河边流浪受孤凄?
痛心事, 莫提起,
家破人亡无消息.
张老三, 莫伤悲,
我的命运不如你!
为什么, 王老七,
你的家乡在何地?
在东北, 做生意,
家乡八年无消息.
这么说, 我和你,
都是有家不能回!
仇和恨, 在心里,
奔腾如同黄河水!
黄河边, 定主意,
咱们一同打回去!
为国家, 当兵去,
太行山上打游击!
从今后, 我和你
一同打回老家去!

六 黄河怨 （女声独唱）

（朗诵词）
朋友！
我们要打回老家去!
老家已经太不成话了!
谁没有妻子儿女,
谁能忍受敌人的欺凌?
亲爱的同胞们!
你听听
一个妇人悲惨的歌声.

丈夫啊,
在天边!
地下啊,
再团圆!
你要想想妻子儿女死得这样惨!
你要替我把这笔血债清算!
你要替我把这笔血债清还!

（歌词）
风啊,
你不要叫喊!
云啊,
你不要躲闪!
黄河啊,
你不要呜咽!
今晚,
我在你面前
哭诉我的愁和冤.
命啊,
这样苦!
生活啊,
这样难!
鬼子啊,
你这样没心肝!
宝贝啊,
你死得这样惨!
我和你无仇又无冤,
偏让我无颜偷生在人间!
狂风啊,
你不要叫喊！
乌云啊,
你不要躲闪,
黄河的水啊,
你不要呜咽！
今晚
我要投在你的怀中,
洗清我的千重愁来万重冤!

七 保卫黄河 （轮唱）

（朗诵词）
但是，
中华民族的儿女啊,
谁愿意像猪羊一般
任人宰割?
我们抱定必胜的决心,
保卫黄河!
保卫华北!
保卫全中国!

（歌词）
风在吼.
马在叫.
黄河在咆哮.
黄河在咆哮.
河西山冈万丈高.
河东河北
高粱熟了.
万山丛中,
抗日英雄真不少!
青纱帐里,
游击健儿逞英豪!
端起了土枪洋枪,
挥动着大刀长矛,
保卫家乡!
保卫黄河!
保卫华北!
保卫全中国!

八 怒吼吧! 黄河！ （大合唱）

（朗诵词）
听啊:
珠江在怒吼!
扬子江在怒吼!
啊!黄河!
掀起你的怒涛,
发出你的狂叫,
向着全中国被压迫的人民,
向着全世界被压迫的人民,
发出你战斗的警号吧!

（歌词）
怒吼吧,黄河!
怒吼吧,黄河!
怒吼吧,黄河!
掀起你的怒涛,
发出你的狂叫!
向着全世界的人民,
发出战斗的警号!
啊----!
五千年的民族,
苦难真不少!
铁蹄下的民众,
苦痛受不了!
受不了......!
新中国已经破晓;
四万万五千万民众
已经团结起来,
誓死同把国土保!
你听,你听,你听:
松花江在呼号;
黑龙江在呼号;
珠江发出了英勇的叫啸;
扬子江上
燃遍了抗日的烽火!
啊！黄河！
怒吼吧! 怒吼吧! 怒吼吧!
向着全中国受难的人民,
发出战斗的警号！
向着全世界劳动的人民,
发出战斗的警号！

光未然
一九三九年三月写于延安

KEY PLACES

Laohekou: The town in Hubei province where Guang Weiran was born in 1913.

Manchuria: A province in northern China where the Japanese set up a puppet state called Manchukuo.

Marco Polo Bridge: A stone bridge to the southwest of Beijing. The site of the incident in 1937 that precipitated war between China and Japan.

Shanghai International Settlement: In Shanghai, the merged British and American settlements.

Wuhan: The new center for cultural activism following the fall of Shanghai.

Yan'an: A town in Shaanxi province where the Long March ended, and site of the Communist Party's headquarters from 1935 to 1948.

KEY DATES

May 30, 1925: British police in Shanghai opened fire on students protesting foreign privileges in China.

1927: When right-wing factions in the Nationalist government began a nationwide crackdown on the CPC.

September 18, 1931: The Manchurian Incident. The Japanese invasion of Manchuria.

1934–1935: The Long March. A series of marches from southeastern to northwestern China made by different groups of Communist armies trying to evade Chiang Kai-shek's much larger military. The march ended in Yan'an, Shaanxi province, where the Communists established their base.

1937: In response to the Japanese invasion, the Nationalist and Communist forces joined to form the Second United Front.

July 7, 1937: The incident at Marco Polo Bridge. The beginning of the war between Japan and China, and the Eastern Front of World War II.

1949: The Communists' Red Army defeated the Nationalists. The Nationalists fled to Taiwan under Chiang Kai-shek. The People's Republic of China was established under Mao Zedong and the Communist Party of China.

Photo Credits and Source Notes

Photograph on page 1: A photograph of my family taken at our home in 1961. I am in the middle.

Photograph on title page: Band members rehearsing *Yellow River Cantata*.

All images courtesy of the author except for the following: page 7 #VCG111134754195 — photo © by Visual China Group; page 13 source unknown / Wikimedia Commons / Public Domain; page 18 (top) #VCG11449495471 — photo © by Visual China Group; page 18 (bottom) Asahigraph / Wikimedia Commons / Public Domain; page 19 #VCG11418784363 — Photo © by Visual China Group; page 30 #VCG11482604101 — photo © by Corbis / Visual China Group; page 37 #VCG11449496937 — photo © by Visual China Group; page 51 (sidebar) #VCG111119329999 — photo © by Chen Zhengqing / Visual China Group.

The *Three Character Classic* lesson quoted on page 8 is from *Elementary Chinese — San Tzu Ching*, translated and annotated by Herbert A. Giles. Shanghai: Messrs. Kelly & Walsh, Ld., 1900.

The quote on page 19 "The Long March is a manifesto. ... the Red Army is their only road to liberation" is from page 94 of *On Guerrilla Warfare* by Mao Tse-tung, translated by Samuel B. Griffith. Mineola, New York: Dover Publications, 2005.

Text and illustrations copyright © 2019 by Ange Zhang
English translation of *Yellow River Cantata* copyright © 2019 by Andi Zhang
Published in Canada and the USA in 2019 by Groundwood Books

We gratefully acknowledge for their financial support of our publishing program the Canada Council for the Arts, the Ontario Arts Council and the Government of Canada

Groundwood Books / House of Anansi Press
groundwoodbooks.com

 Canada Council for the Arts   Conseil des Arts du Canada

 ONTARIO ARTS COUNCIL
CONSEIL DES ARTS DE L'ONTARIO
an Ontario government agency
un organisme du gouvernement de l'Ontario

With the participation of the Government of Canada
Avec la participation du gouvernement du Canada | Canadä

Library and Archives Canada Cataloguing in Publication
Title: A song for China : how my father wrote Yellow River cantata / Ange Zhang.
Other titles: How my father wrote Yellow River cantata
Names: Zhang, Ange, author, illustrator.
Description: Text in English; includes English translation of Yellow River Cantata lyrics followed by the original Mandarin.
Identifiers: Canadiana (print) 20189067454 | Canadiana (ebook) 20189067462 | ISBN 9781773061511 (hardcover) | ISBN 9781773061528 (EPUB) | ISBN 9781773062730 (Kindle)
Subjects: LCSH: Guang, Weiran — Juvenile literature. | LCSH: Xian, Xinghai, 1905-1945. Huang He da he chang — Juvenile literature. | LCSH: Poets, Chinese — 20th century — Biography —Juvenile literature. |
LCSH: Yellow River (China) — Songs and music — Juvenile literature. | LCSH: China — History — Republic, 1912-1949 — Juvenile literature. | LCGFT: Biographies.
Classification: LCC PL2763.U26 Z76 2019 | DDC j895.11/5—dc23

The illustrations were done in Photoshop.
Design by Michael Solomon
Map of China by Scott MacNeill
Printed and bound in Malaysia

MIX
Paper from responsible sources
FSC® C012700